A S o u l W a y

O f

F o r g i v e n e s s

R o b e r t S a r d e l l o

A Soul Way of Forgiveness Copyright © 2017 by Robert Sardello

This book is a work of fiction. Names, characters, businesses, organiza- tions,

For information : www.RobertSardello.com

Book and Cover design by Robert Sardello

ISBN: 9781520703145

First Edition: 2017

10 9 8 7 6 5 4 3

With Gratitude to the many inviduals who have taken courses, attended the conferences and soul retreats of the School of Spiritual Pschology from 1992 to 2017. While the School of Spiritual Psychology was released to the spiritual worlds on May 12, 2017, the work will go on through these archives and the individual offerings of Robert Sardello.

A Soul Way of Forgiveness

Robert Sardello, Ph.D. taught for many years at the University of Dallas and is a founding fellow of the Dallas Institute of Humanities and Culture. With Cheryl Sanders-Sardello, he founded the School of Spiritual Psychology in 1992. The school offers soul retreats and courses at various locations throughout the world, online courses, and spiritual pilgrimages to significant known and unknown holy places. He is the author of eight books, including ***Love and the Soul: Creating a Future for Earth***,***Silence: the Mystery of Wholeness***; and ***Heartfulness***.

www.RobertSardello.com

Introduction

This monograph develops practical understanding and methods of forgiveness – of ourselves, of others, and as the most powerful of world-forces. We enter into an entirely new and creative way of working with **Forgiveness. Forgiving, we discover, is a particular region of the soul, a Presence** – an interior landscape, and the Presence of healing Presences. **The inner contemplative work is to be able to locate this region.** As long as we attempt forgiveness from the place of usual consciousness, we lock ourselves into subtle modes of power through separating ourselves from the soul being of those we wish to forgive.

We look at why forgiveness is of importance and as perhaps the deepest mystery of the soul. It is most certainly the only way to move out of the patterns of repetitious harmfulness we live both individually **and the harmfulness characterizing these times.**

We listen with and to our soul and try to feel how the illusory benefits, often unconscious and very powerful, often prevents attempts to forgive. We then examine the ill effects of living with resentment in our emotional, physical and spiritual life. We look at what harming others and being harmed by others does to the soul.

We develop here the nature of forgiveness as requiring the development of new soul capacities, and ways to identify and develop these modes of imagination through contemplative practicesractical aspects of this writing.

Perhaps nothing counts as more important in this time than learning the art and the practice of forgiveness. In the past several decade, for example, the United States has suffered incredible catastrophes – the Oklahoma City Bombing, a boming of the World Trade Center, a second boming of the World Trade Center which killed over 2000 peoples. And, the United States retaliated this destruction by meeting it with war. This country has two great lacks – we do not know how to grieve, and we do not know how to enter into the process of forgiveness. The two are intimately related. The opposite of grieve is greed. Greed is the great pretence of attempting to forget death with a false kind of immortality, the accumulation of more and more. Because we cannot grieve, we cannot forgive.

A Soul Way of Forgiveness
Robert Sardello

Why a new understanding of forgiveness is essential for our time

The deepest understanding of forgiveness requires a turn of thought that is nothing short of courageous. Namely, it entails delving into the most tragic aspects of human relationships, the horrifically painful things that make us feel separate, isolated, and alone. And the forms these issues take are innumerable. The aftermath of emotional dysfunction includes anger, resentment, hurt, haunting memories, and, in short, the things that make us feel injured by others. Plus, we must also give attention to ostensibly loving relationships that, in fact, are unspoken contracts, bargains struck to banish pain that was present long before a relationship began. Additionally, it's also important to examine the multiple ways in which we engage in psychological and spiritual self-harm.

These various iterations of pain likely account for eighty percent of contemporary visits to therapists, support groups, and healers of various sorts. The popularity and continuance of work begun by John Bradshaw, Melody Beattie, Robert Bly and many others can be attributed to their ability to parse feelings of victimization. After all, we're a victim society. It might be said, too, that those who offer to heal pain are handsomely paid for their advice, indicating the sheer desperation and ardent desire for relief from emotional afflictions.

Nearly everyone has suffered some abuse — physical, emotional, sexual, spiritual, etc. And the corollary is a horrifying uptick in addictions of every variety. Drugs, sex, love, emotion, money, and power not only account for the ways we get stuck in our lives; they also inevitably point towards an occurrence of victimization. Thus, intimate relationships and the difficulties they entail, such as infidelities, indifference, fighting, anger, and resentment, can be attributed to soul-pain brought into a relationship along with the illusion that the relationship will offer a solution to that pain. And, lastly, there's the anger and resentment toward those who exercise authority over us — in work, religion, and even in government.

A large and exciting new expanse of life opens when we look meditatively upon the phenomenon of being a victim — without judging it or excusing it because "life is hard." Victimization is a symptom, pointing to something that hasn't yet found expression. Thus, it's helpful
to accept that we're all victims, and we're also victimizers. And this realization reveals a path to health, one that allows for movement to finally emerge. And that movement is *forgiveness.*

Moreover, the issues surrounding harm done to ourselves and others transcend individual relating. Racial prejudice, exploitation of the planet's natural resources, rampant nationalism, crime, greed, and the struggle of women throughout the world are only a few examples. Moreover, these grievous wrongs are not only going unchecked; astonishingly, they're rapidly increasing. Since there are no feelings of conscience or guilt to impede cruel behavior, *we* desperately need forgiveness for our wounded — and wounding — culture.

Currently, it's fashionable to see incidences of rampant violence and harm as signs of moral breakdown. At least that is the stance taken by political conservatives, and they find the idea of returning o an imaginary past to be a viable means of addressing these difficult issues. While ideas of religion, family, and tradition are part of their proposed ethos, a more thoughtful point of view makes us pause and see the situation differently. Namely, humanity is engaged in reconfiguring cultural ideas that should be broadly embraced.

And perhaps it may be that there isn't a greater occurrence of cruelty in the world; instead, we simply may be more aware due to media. Thus, what's genuinely new is our vision. And it must be hoped that we, like Shakespeare's King Lear, have finally learned "to see better." Thus, while the occurrence of violent episodes is *more* frequently noticed, we can now exercise new ways of dealing with their wounding presence.

Accepting this newly acquired emotional terrain is nothing less than a ratcheting up of psychic evolution and, luckily, it has a familiar name. Quite simply, it's called *forgiveness.*

Why forgiveness requires a new form of consciousness

We already have certain assumptions concerning forgiveness. After all, it's a common word. But it requires a dramatic shift to realize that typical meanings of this word have little to do with reality.

"I" can never forgive someone — it's not within the power of ego consciousness to banish the effect of harm. In fact, the ego is the very bearer of the memory of the harm we've experienced; thus, to dissolve these memories, the ego would have to dissolve itself. And the ego makes it possible for us to get on in the world at all. What's particularly heartening about the aforementioned new consciousness beginning to emerge is that it's not oriented towards destroying the ego, but transforming it.

We already have certain assumptions concerning forgiveness. After all, it's a common word. But it requires a dramatic shift to realize that typical meanings of this word have little to do with reality.

From the viewpoint of spiritual psychology, what must arise is a means of transforming the ego without harming it.

False forgiveness

As stated, the ego is the bearer of memories, and it's due to memory that we have a sense of identity

.

Thus, to *decide* to forgive someone bears within the decision itself an innate inadequacy. Forgiveness can turn into an act of power and be translated into the following:

"You're a terrible person because of what you have done to hurt me, and I'm an innocent victim of your unjustified attack. But, in the goodness of my heart, I forgive you." This is false forgiveness. Still, there are instances in which it seems we have nothing to do with the harm that has befallen us.

For example, it's impossible to imagine that a small child has played any part in, say, being brutally beaten by a parent. When such a child grows up and suffers the scars of abuse, the primary realm where forgiveness needs to take place, though, is not towards the parent, but towards oneself. Why? Because, to live with the soul pain of the abuse, the child, and even as an adult, does all sorts of harm to himself/herself to attempt to live normally." Even here, however, it's not possible to forgive oneself from an egocentric perspective. Instead, the question of forgiveness must be framed rightly.

Understanding the ego

The ego thwarts the possibility of forgiveness since it's so closely aligned with our sense of personal identity. Our sense of self emerges from the necessary developmental process of separating ourselves from others and from our surroundings. In essence, it poses the question, " Who am I?" And the answer comes in the fundamental form of memories.

Everything that has happened to us operates as a vital sense of the ego. The second aspect of ego is our conscious ways of construing the world — and the mode of imagination enacted by the ego confers a sense of literalism. What the ego imagines is taken to be real and operates with strict singularity.

While it's very comfortable to have a sense of yourself, this separation is accompanied by a deep feeling of guilt that isn't personal in nature. Instead, it's metaphysical guilt that's part of the human condition. Religions sometimes refer to this omnipresent sense of guilt as a post-lapsarian state and, while it's perennially present, we don't consciously feel it all of the time. The ego also deploys mechanisms that shield us from it — unless we have been harmed by someone. At that point, guilt intensifies. For example, individuals who have been robbed feel violated, but they also feel guilt! Astonishingly, even a person who has been assaulted also feels guilt.

In our state of separateness, we perceive everything that is "other" as a threat. We already feel small, helpless, and subject to annihilation; after all, the ego, in relation to everything else — both within and without — looms quite small. Thus, the cost of having a personal identity is huge. In essence, it's agreement to live in fear.

Ego maintenance

For the ego to maintain itself, it necessarily creates the illusion that the ego can solve the problems of its guilt and fear; this is interesting because it means that the ego is much more than an expression of personal identity. Rather, it's a function, a function of consciousness that structures the way we see the world.

It's also pervaded with a kind of intelligence, although we're not conscious of it, that's thoroughly capable of denying guilt and fear. Psychoanalytic psychology has come up with a list of about fifty different kinds of "ego defense mechanisms," which means there are many iterations of denial. And the use of the metaphor of "mechanisms" is fascinating. The word implies that there's no consciousness in denial. And yet, this consciousness *is* intelligent; in fact, it's so intelligent that it continually morphs into an infinite variety of forms. There's something in us that far outstrips our capacity for intelligence. And this lack of consciousness implies intelligence that's beyond the 'usual'-human; perhaps it's a sub-nature that operates invisibly.

Once we glimpse this capacity for denial, we can begin to observe it from the standpoint of our "I." And, again, when we feel harmed by someone, we become aware of our separateness. To not feel the guilt and fear of that separateness, we accuse others of causing our uffering; we only see that aspect, not the aspect of our denial mechanisms. Further, we find ourselves feeling that this person must be punished.

Others, then, are ostensibly the cause of our suffering. "If my parents had not been so cruel, I would be able to live happily." Or, in a larger scale, "If others weren't evil, then I wouldn't suffer!" If you remember the nationally televised memorial service after the Oklahoma bombing, and every such tragedy since, "forgiveness" wasn't mentioned one time, not even by Billy Graham. Nor has it been mentioned after all other acts of terrorism since. Thus, we missed a tremendous opportunity for healing. But the ego always needs an enemy. And, sometimes, the one who seems to cause our suffering is ourself. "If I were only smarter, I wouldn't have failed the course."

Another prevalent means the ego finds to avoid the experience of guilt is by looking for a cause with which to establish a "special" love. Guilt is a feeling of lack, a feeling that there is something wrong with me, and there must be a person who can prove that I'm worthwhile. In turn, I can verify for this person that he or she is also worthwhile. An implicit contract is made. "As long as you act in such a way that my needs are met (and I can avoid my guilt), I will help you avoid your pain by fulfilling your needs. But if you change and don't do what I expect, then I will accuse you of not caring for me. In this relationship, if I ever feel bad, it's your fault!"

All of this has been recognized by modern psychology and has become standard fare in the inner child movement and twelve-step programs. Alice Miller, the founder of all of the current models of psychological thinking regarding harm, speaks out against forgiveness. In the 1994 revised edition of *The Drama of the Gifted Child*, she says:

"My own experience has taught me that the enactment of forgiveness — which sixteen years ago, I still believed to be right — brings the
*therapeutic process to a halt. It blocks the unfolding of feelings and perceptions that are impossible to experience at the early stages of therapy, but that, with an increase in inner strength and resilience, can eventually be faced. Some memories surface years after the beginning of self-therapy, when we have finally become strong enough to face them. **This fruitful surfacing of new memories must not be hindered by the closure that forgiveness would produce.**" (p. 21)*

Alice Miller is correct; it's not possible to forgive someone from the confines of the ego. And for her, the therapeutic process involves gradually coming to "forgotten" memories after one has undergone a strengthening of the ego. But, once the memories surface, it becomes impossible to enter into forgiveness, though it seems possible to "forgive" due to an emboldened form of a (more "fixed") ego. Again, this sort of therapy makes forgiveness impossible.

Feeling as a new basis for forgiveness

Anxiety (doubt)

Therapeutic concern exits about the effects of abuse in early childhood, primarily physical abuse. But we should also include other forms of harm. And it doesn't have to originate in childhood. A man who beats his wife, or anyone who has been physically assaulted — all physical attacks — are violations of the sense of touch.

Thus, it's fruitful to explore the sense of touch and what it means when ruptured by an imbalance.

The organ for the sense of touch is skin, the surface of the body. When we touch something or are touched, the primary sensation comes about through a sense of movement. Touch throws us back into the sensation of our body —and, through feeling our body, we simultaneously discover the world. For example, if I touch a piece of wood or a nail, what I experience is <u>resistance</u>. My skin presses inward. If something touches my skin with force, I feel pain. Through touch, we sense our bodily nature, and this happens in ways that make it clear that my bodily nature is different from the world around me.

Also, touch is only a dim impression of resistance. We know there's something different "against" us and this difference reminds us of our bodily being. We're forced to meet the world as "other" — and, with the sense of touch alone, the character of this other thing can't fully be known.

While the surface of the body is the organ of touch, touch often extends beyond the body. For example, if I write with a piece of chalk, I not only feel my body at the place where my fingers curl around the chalk, I also feel my body where the point of the chalk touches the blackboard. Similarly, if I walk with a cane, I feel my body where my fingers grasp the cane, but I also feel the place where the cane touches the earth. Now, let us explore the sense of touch even more deeply.

The sense of touch gives us the most immediate and crude sense of the world as something apart from our body. But, just as importantly, the world is felt from within us. Thus, touch is an inner sense.

If something impresses itself upon us too strongly, we don't merely have an inner sense of it as something other than our body. Instead, we acutely feel our body in a state of shock. At first, it's not even pain, which emerges later. When touching occurs in this way, the delicate contour of the inner sense of touch is disturbed. If you have ever been hit forcefully, try to remember the moment of impact. Now, press the thumb of your left hand into the palm of your right hand, and notice the sensation. Compare this feeling with what you remember when hit. Or, make a fist with your left hand and slam it into your right hand. The first sensation is distinctly pleasurable. The second, we can't really call pain — again, that comes later. Instead, you feel your own body as an object.

To feel our own body as an object — and, of course, it isn't — is to be thrown into a living experience of bodily death. It's as if the life force has been squeezed out of the body. This means we have a momentary experience of our body as a corpse. The aftermath of such an experience is anxiety, which subsequently begins to live in the body. Put succinctly; it's not the content of the memory of violence that's most damaging. If it were just content, forgiveness would come easily. But something far deeper has occurred. Harm abruptly introduces us to death.

Anxiety, then, is a bodily experience, and it's also a memory of a death experience. And the essence of the death experience is that our body is separate from an ongoing connection with the world, a connection we weren't even aware of, but is always happening within the flow of life.

It should be noted that all of this addresses harm of the physical body, but it also applies to emotional, and spiritual "blows."

Forgiveness and bodily anxiety

Living with enormous bodily anxiety requires working to heal the feeling of isolation from the physical world. Thus, much more is involved than merely recovering the memory of trauma. Someone who lives in bodily anxiety no longer relates comfortably with the world; instead, they're trying to absorb the whole of the world into themselves in a wrong-headed effort to ensure safety. This might take the form of "acquiring" the world by eating; avidly seeking comfort; or an overwhelming need for material things.

Someone who has suffered a physical attack, whether as a child or an adult, no longer trusts the world as an intimate partner in life. Outside a therapeutic setting, when I listen to descriptions of people who have suffred attack, I often hear interesting stories of how people dealt with their wounding experience. The most fascinating people are those who didn't resort to therapy but worked through the difficulty themselves. Many times, they spent a great deal of time alone, often in the natural world.

They also frequently began working with nature and began gardening, or growing flowers. Sometimes this would evolve into an interest in healing herbs. They also became far more aware of the cycles of the seasons. Beautiful minerals and crystals also intrigued some of them. Still, others become extraordinarily interested in the care of animals. And it's important not to view all of this from the viewpoint of psychological theory. These people are intuitively engaging in the process of forgiveness.

In all of these cases, immediate sensory awareness heals a rupture in one's ability to live easily in the world. Also, these people don't become recluses; rather, they gradually begin to trust people again. There are certainly other factors to take into account, but learning to trust the physical world is an auspicious beginning. In the case of a physical attack, a disturbance begins in the sentient body and there is grave danger that the physical body will harden and lack the supple characteristics needed to interact with nature and the world as a whole. Further, a spontaneous move towards the natural world for healing offers a vivifying spiritual dimension. All of the planet, including vegetation, animals, and minerals is filled with helpful spiritual beings, usually referred to as elemental beings or devas. Every single plant has a guardian being, a deva, and this is true throughout the natural world. When we work in loving ways with the natural world, these guardian beings become helpful to us.

People who have been terribly harmed by others lose the nuanced balance involved in the sense of touch — the exchange of sensing one's body while simultaneously experiencing the otherness of the world.
Without this restorative experience, it's impossible to work at a soul level. In fact, soul experience can only follow healthy embodiment. Otherwise, disembodied soul work will ensue. It may be fascinating, but it will also only be an abstraction. Thus, establishing healthy connections with the physical world awakens us beautifully and wholly.

Fear and shame

When a person experiences harm, touch isn't the only sense that's impaired. The soul of someone harmed fills with images of pain. When such images surface, the ego turns them into fantasies of anger, resentment, and retaliation. While the soul suffers through pain, the ego fervently desires to do something to rectify the harm felt. The ego is invested the illusory notion that it can destroy the pain.

However, trying to annihilate what lives in the soul as images of pain is impossible. On the contrary, it traps one in the past. And, in becoming preoccupied with the past, the ego doesn't allow new images of what's coming forth from the future. Thus, we become victims yet again — victims of fate, unable to experience a unique and exciting sense of destiny. One becomes incapable of perceiving what's unfolding in the present. It's as if the ego is saying, "Avoid experiencing what's here right now; it's not important. What's important is eradicating the past." Erasing our past, of course, is impossible and, thus, far from freeing us from the past, it condemns us to perpetually reside in it. The corollary is decidedly unpleasant — dwelling in the present is relegated to living in a state of complete and utter negativity.

The images of pain living in the soul of someone who has been harmed don't primarily have to do with the content of memories. Rather, it's the quality of these images that convey an overwhelming feeling of pain that take on the guise of fear and shame. Fear and shame have to do with a disturbance of the life sense. The life sense is not recognized as a sense by current psychology, but it is one of the twelve senses described by Rudolf Steiner, the originator of the metaphysical system of Anthroposophy, and it's also one of the inner senses.

The life sense gives us an inner sensation of our body. Ordinarily, this sense has to do with the harmonious interaction among all the organs of the body, which expresses itself as the feeling of life that is present throughout waking consciousness. It's felt like a quality of well-being. Usually, we're not aware of this sense because it functions continuously. Through this sense, we experience ourselves as part of our physical body. Only when there is bodily disturbance does this sense come to our attention. For example, pain, hunger, thirst, depression, misery are experiences of the life sense when it is out of balance. As an aside, schizophrenia, among other things, is a profound disturbance of the life sense in which one is unable to identify with one's body.

The organs of the life sense are the sympathetic and parasympathetic nervous systems. The sympathetic nervous system is connected with fear. When we experience fear, for example, the pupils of our eyes widen, our face turns white with tension, our intestines and stomach cramp, and our heart speeds up. This kind of reaction of the sympathetic nervous system is an indication of ultimate bodily fear, the fear of death. The parasympathetic nervous system, however, is connected with shame. When we experience shame, our pupils narrow, our skin blushes, our heart slows, and we feel sensations of warmth. Shame is the body's attempt to hide; it can even become a bodily "wish" that we had never been born.

Fear and shame are basic emotions of human existence. As long as we're connected to the world and have a trust of the world and others, we don't feel these emotions in an unbalanced manner. Being harmed by someone isn't the cause of fear and shame, but, instead, it's a condition under which these emotions are strongly felt without any warning.

When fear and shame are aroused, emotional and cognitive development is affected. The sympathetic nervous system, when affected by fear over a period of time, expresses itself as an impulse towards perfectionism. We feel an uncontrollable need to be perfect — and, since this isn't possible, we're reduced to living in a state of fear. Interestingly, the parasympathetic nervous system has a direct connection to our sexual organs. When the parasympathetic system is over-activated one might feel strong sexual shame or, alternately, a very strong sexual drive, behind which shame is sure to lurk.

Forgiveness and the life sense

An imbalance of the life sense presents issues with simply being 'at home in our skin" without undue feelings of imperfection or shame. When the life sense is out of balance, it feels impossible to address the situation — all that is felt is bodily uneasiness. The soul experiences suffering; however, the ego tries desperately to address the situation. Thus, I can't be with myself outside of my ego without becoming egotistical. The popular work on healing the inner child provides a means of healing fear and shame. But, in that context, one has to first form an inner image of oneself as a child and subsequently learn to care for the child. But where does the capacity for caring for the inner child come from? Such a capacity might rightly be called compassion. But much of the work with the inner child is understood to mean that I, in my ego consciousness, resolve to care for the wounded child. A lack of clarity in this regard leads to fostering unhealthy and rampant egotism.

The ego can remember, but it cannot imagine. If I remember being wounded as a child, it's the soul that creates an image of the inner child. In doing so, the soul may need the assistance of the ego, but the actual image issues from the soul. So, the most important aspect of inner child work concerns the act of making inner images.

In the making of the image, I am "holding" my woundedness — and that's an act of compassion. This act of compassion is tremendously important. And it's meaningful not because I'm caring for myself — but because I'm learning to care for another via an image. For instance, when an image of myself is experienced, it's actually, phenomenologically speaking, functioning as another person. With this understanding, it's possible to gradually begin practicing compassion for others. I'm able to feel what another person feels, and able to be with him/her no matter what they're feeling. And this ability to be with others serves to restore my being.

Forgiveness and soul life

The soul as experienced in waking life is quite different from the experience of the soul in depth psychology. Rather than focus on the unconscious, I want to explore soul life in full consciousness in order to address forgiveness more fully. As we proceed, this will become clearer, and, forgiveness is only possible through the development of a consciously vital soul life.

The soul gives us a sense of an interior life that is more than 'me' and yet is intimately interwoven with the 'I' and it is the interior qualities of experience that affect our relationships with others and the world. In depth psychology the emphasis is solely on the interior life and, thus, it lacks an understanding of how soul is oriented towards both the self and the world.

Soul "breathes" in the world through sensations and perceptions. For example, seeing a rose is an act of sensation. But I can then turn away from the actual bloom and notice an inner image of it. That inner image is never neutral. Whatever is taken in and becomes an interior experience bifurcates into two qualities, likes and dislikes — or a sense of antipathy that's in opposition to sympathy. For the soul, nothing is neutral; the soul is in dynamic movement, constantly weaving polarities into images.

The movement between likes and dislikes gives the soul proof of its own existence, and this "proof" is reflected in the richness of images that fleetingly become conscious; for the most part, we're unaware of these images. This level of soul life, where inner images of the world dwell, is the sentient soul.

The effects of harm on the sentient soul

Trauma disrupts the soul's ability to interweave images in healthy ways. This is why traumatic events often can't be remembered. Typical psychological explanations for this are deemed as a kind of protective mechanism. But that's a fallacy; in fact, there's no memory at all because there's no image of the occurrence.

Instead, there's an imbalance, either on the side of antipathy or the side of sympathy. For example, physical harm may cause the soul to gravitate towards antipathy and, at that point, the soul is seized by rigidity and fixed ideas. Ways this might be expressed include: "I can't stand to be touched." Or: "Feelings are just too painful to experience!"

However, if the sentient soul is weighted on the side of sympathy, the soul then seeks out experiences in which its activities cause sensational reactions — both to oneself and to others. One example of this one-sidedness is the phenomenon of co-dependency. For example, someone will say, "I need to be touched," but any attempts to do so will be met with absolute rejection. "How dare you touch me. This inner contradiction arises from anxiety and confusion.

Balance in sentient soul life is necessary for forgiveness to occur.

Souls caught in antipathy and sympathy need an abundance of image experiences. But how is it possible to develop one's capacity for images?

One way is to begin paying attention to dream life; it's important not to interpret the dreams or try to explain them. Simply recall the dream, tell them as stories, and feel their textural qualities.

Yet another way might be to spend time each day consciously making an inner image of something experienced that day:
- of something beautiful in the natural world
- of the qualities of different plants
- of the movements and actions of an animal
- of human beings — the way an individual walks; facial expressions

I don't mean simply observing things of the world; rather, make an inner image after the "event" and hold the image for a few minutes. This relates to trauma in the following way: when one has been harmed, the capacity for imagination isn't present. It must be consciously developed.

onsciously developing the capacity of imagination is a necessary
ep in the process of forgiveness. It restores the soul's connection
 the world. It does no good whatsoever to simply tell someone
at you forgive them. Nor does it do any good to *decide* to forgive
meone. Instead, one must take up something consciously that
ould have been natural before the occurrence of trauma.

houghtful forgiveness: Harm and the capacity to think

eople who have been harmed have difficulty thinking in healthy
ays. I'm not referring to the content of thought, but the very act
 thinking itself. Thinking is a soul activity. For most of us,
owever, it's *not* a soul activity because we tend to think already
ought thoughts rather than enter into the creative thinking
ctivity and this is an indication that, as a culture, we've endured
emendous suffering.

leas are images; in fact, the word itself comes from the Greek,
idos, meaning image. However, most of us don't think in images,
id this is nothing less than a strident indication of ruptures in
motion, thought and soul life.

he sentient soul, we've observed, is enlivened by polarities of
ntipathy and sympathy — and, in a healthful state, the interplay
aakes inner images. Healthy soul thinking consists of the
iterweaving of polarities and, thus, allows for subtle differences
etween one idea and another. And, importantly, this healthy mode
f soul-thinking makes it possible to remain focused on the
whole" of what is being considered while also remaining attentive
 details. It's appropriate to also refer to this activity as imaginal
iinking.

Importantly, an effect of suffering harm becomes evident in a disruption of one's capacity for imaginal thinking. Thinking becomes unbalanced, and a capacity for differentiation devolves into abstraction. In this case, only one aspect of something is seen, and that singular aspect must be deemed true. This one-sidedness also shows up in the way individuals think about the harm done to them in the past. "I know now that my father abused me. All men are to be distrusted." It should be noted, though, that it's not only through such suffering that thinking becomes disrupted. Education also greatly harms the soul when imaginal thought is dismissed in favor of thinking that's solely intellectual (abstract).

An unbalanced sympathy of the soul can also breed fanaticism.

For example: "My parents abused me. I will never marry and have children. No one should ever marry." In this case, thinking is supplanted by overwhelming feeling; however, the feeling is expressed in the guise of an odd brand of logic.

Healing the divided soul of thinking

Imaginal thinking allows for the simultaneous appreciation of attention and differentiation. Abstraction and fanaticism, on the other hand, become evident when intellectual concerns circumvent perception. In the case of abstraction, the world of concepts becomes cold and devoid of the health that is conferred upon us by feeling.

Also, fanaticism ruptures thinking by clouding it with feeling. In this case, feeling pain is so great that it can only be individualized and personal; attention is so fixed on one's pain that thinking becomes murky. Fanaticism colors the capacity of the soul in ways hat make it revolve solely around the self and, moreover, it's a rapped version of self that has suffered great diminution. Attention, in this context, is overly focused on the inner aspects of the soul.

n both abstraction and fanaticism, the soul no longer welcomes what's presented in the phenomena of the world. If the polarity within the sentient soul isn't stabilized by working on the capacity for image-making, then a splintering of the soul will become evident in thinking. In fact, if the senses of touch and life aren't carefully healed, then the possibility for soul life itself is occluded.

And the soul life of thinking can't be healed except by loving the sentient body and the sentient soul in ways that cultivate an ability to make and hold inner images.

Referring to "making and holding" images can wrongly convey a notion that images are static. Instead, they're constantly forming and evolving. In order to make and hold an inner image, the will has to *actively* make the image. Moreover, one has to concentrate attention on the image — and that is truly an act of creation. To develop the creative act of imaginal thinking, an exercise can be practiced:

Visualize a circle. If this proves difficult, pretend you are standing in front of a blackboard. See your hand draw the circle on the blackboard. Focus now on the circle until it fades away. If the circle moves, look with your eyes closed in the direction in which the circle has moved away. Focus your eyes in this direction, then move them slowly back to the center. Again, see your hand drawing the circle. Focus on the circle until it fades away. After the exercise, cover a piece of paper with circles you draw. Draw as many as possible. It's the movement we're after, not the drawing itself. This kind of exercise develops the capacity to experience images as constantly active and perpetually in the process of being formed. The development of this capacity strengthens the ability for mobile thinking, which is soul thinking.

The interweaving of the polarities of differentiation and attention can be characterized as "warm thinking." We have empathy with whatever we focus upon — sympathy (attention) becomes empathy, and we notice subtle differences. Thus, our thinking becomes nuanced (antipathy, or differentiation). This kind of thinking is quite different than what we customarily engage in. It's a kind of thinking that doesn't overstep its bounds or engage in judgment. Soul thinking, heart thinking, brings order without resorting to narrow conclusions. It's also a living being that is perennially revealing itself. Thinking in terms of conclusions is dead thought; its rigidity is so stringent that it's utterly opposed to the vitality present in the stream of life.

The healing of thinking is essential to the process of forgiveness. To think in the style of the polarities of abstraction or fanaticism — which is also fundamentalism — are expressions of fear. And the attempt to conquer fear easily moves us towards a need for control and, at that point, thinking ceases to be a soul activity. A tremendously important step in coming to forgiveness is giving up. This single step helps restore us to the living activity of the world, of which we are a vital and loving part.

Receiving forgiveness

Forgiveness poses paradoxes. We're unable to bring it about but we, nonetheless, must ready ourselves for it by balancing and healing body-soul-thinking. In a very real sense, we're working on forgiving ourselves; however, we're also preparing for the possibility of being receptive to inspiration issuing from the spiritual world.

A further paradox is apparent: in order to be receptive to inspiration, we must intensely work on ourselves in the ways discussed in the previous text. And then we must concentrate, without effort, on attempts to become an open, empty vessel that is capable of "conceiving," so to speak. The work of preparing body-soul-thinking, thus, is oriented towards a "birthing" of the soul rather than the achievement of specific, measurable results. The exercises must be exercised in an inner way to develop the powers of the will— and it must be developed in such a way that allows us to experience moments in which we make our inner life an empty vessel. Practically speaking, this means that I spend ten minutes each day sitting in silence, emptying all conscious thoughts, feelings, and imagination. This is a gradual process of soul purification.

If we're able to experience moments of emptiness, the soul gradually develops a new capacity, the capacity of feeling-knowing. This capacity is analogous to the bodily sensation of touch. In fact, it could be called spiritual touch. Inspiration is felt as a subtle soul sense of touch. The experience of spiritual touch is a feeling-knowing that isn't intellectual, yet it carries certainty because we're in touch with spiritual realms. This connection doesn't take place in the form of receiving information; it's more like being touched by an invisible.

In the practice of making an inner image of something that has occurred during the day, for example, one begins to feel a kind of firmness in the region of the forehead.

An important aspect of this exercise in noticing is to focus on that feeling of firmness and then move the current of feeling up over the head and down the spine. This aspect of the exercise is important. Moving the current over the head and down the spine brings the current of inspiration into the organs of the body.

One effect of feeling the flow of inspiration is that we gradually realize that any harm done to us belongs to the past. We may have known this all along, but that intellectual knowing has no real effect. This new feeling-knowing is very effective because spiritual touch takes us into a different time current, the time current of the future. We gradually become more interested, more engaged in the possibilities of our future, while remaining fully sensorily in the 'now,' rather than what has happened to us in the past. And this experience is *not* in the realm of fantasy.

We don't suddenly begin imagining ourselves doing things we never thought we could. Feeling-knowing, instead, is a feeling of being drawn towards something. The content of what we're being drawn towards isn't given. Rather than receiving content, we begin to experience the unfolding of our own being. At times, when we feel blocked or are drawn back into familiar patterns, the feeling of being pulled forward becomes even more pronounced — because we momentarily lost it. The work now becomes one of staying in touch with that current of feeling-knowing. Gradually, we begin to realize that there are things to be known that we simply can't apprehend through the intellect. Thus, it's wise to trust this new way of knowing-feeling.

Forgiveness as a life process

Forgiveness isn't an action, a one-time decision. It's a process of coming to new ways of knowing and being. Forgiveness actually has very little to do with focusing on memories of how and by whom we've been harmed. In fact, that kind of thinking will allow those who have harmed us to control our sense of ourselves and our destiny. Instead of making our images, we're filled with obsessive images of the past. The process of forgiveness, on the other hand, is oriented towards bringing our consciousness as a healing force into the world.

But what about our wounds? What happens to them?

Listening — the other side of forgiveness

Once we experience the subtle touch of feeling-knowing, an even further dimension of knowing becomes available. While the current of inspiration is felt as coming from outside — as a light presence of a subtle form of touch, a second non-intellectual knowing originates from our very deepest self. Johann Wolfgang von Goethe called this realm "dark ideas," and his character, Faust, refers to it as "the Mothers."

This new dimension of knowing comes from working to develop the heart-soul. When one works to heal the split between thinking that is abstract and thinking that is too feeling filled, what we called fanaticism, the heart-soul begins to develop.
Thinking that begins to be felt more in the region of the heart rather than the head, imaginal thinking, can be experienced more strongly. An important means of expanding thinking in the region of the heart is to send heart-feelings from the central region of the body out to the periphery of the body — from the heart, through

the deep interior of the body, toward the arms, hands, and limbs.

In working to develop the forces of the heart, the wounds of the soul, the wounds of the past are forgotten. However, they aren't lost; instead, they drop like seeds into a fertile womb of darkness. They're the seeds for a new capacity of knowing, which is highly intuitive. And intuition, as experienced in the soul life, is analogous to hearing. It's an inner listening.

What is heard through intuition

Hearing is an appropriate analogy for intuition or the manner in which it's received. Hearing gives us intimate knowledge, a sense of knowing something from the inside. As long as we're caught in memories of harm done to us, we remain external observers, looking at what happened to us. We don't know our wounds intimately in that we can't hear what they have to tell us. Hearing gives the interior qualities of things; for example, the sound of striking a metal object versus a wooden object. We know the difference through sound because something of the interior of each thing struck expresses its being.

What is "heard" resounds in a subtle way from the interior of soul life. This quality of intuition is ineffable. In describing some of what is heard, it must be realized that I'm giving words to something that has only tonal soul qualities. The words come later, as insights emerging from the darkness:

One. We begin to hear the fatigue of the soul; we begin to hear the malaise of the soul; this fatigue and malaise are heard as resounding not just in my soul **- but also as the soul condition** of humanity at this time.

Two. Through hearing the fatigue of the soul, there's an inner recognition that the structures governing the world are now abusive. In fact, they destroy the imaginal capacities of the soul.

Three. What used to be experienced as my personal failures, all my feelings of being unable to operate in the world as effectively as others do, can be more objectively perceived as an inevitable decline and collapse of old structures and forms in the world. And "success" is usually an illusion based upon a denial of soul life. Thus, my so-called personal failures (which I attributed to harm inflicted upon me by others) can now be heard as part of the demise of a rapidly collapsing world.

Four. What is also heard is: the decline of a world based upon a denial of soul urges one towards self-indulgence. All the addictions and attractions to success, defined materially, aren't merely ways of denying personal pain — they're *fostered* by the dying structures of the world in a strangely contrived means designed to obscure pain.

Five. What is also heard is a voice saying, "There are no real solutions because the problems are too big. Get what you can while you can, for we are at the end."

Six. But there is another side to what intuition hears. A yearning is felt from within, and a new and nurturing space is located — the space of the heart. What is heard from within this space is a yearning to create beauty, harmony, healing, not just for our sake or for aesthetic appeal, but for the healing of the world.

Seven. Additionally, what is heard in intuition is compassion, warmth, and a sense of resolve, an understanding that there's no trial given to us that's beyond endurance. We know this is a living truth because we have lived through the trial of severe harm, and the purpose of our trials was to develop new ways of thinking, feeling, and acting in (and for) the world.

Forgiving as an act of love: The subtle qualities of forgiveness

One. Forgiving as an act of love is felt, not achieved. It can be given, but it can't be bestowed as an act of triumph over another person, which would humiliate the other person. Forgiveness is a means of releasing yourself and others from an experience of hurt, injury, wounding, suffering, humiliation or pain that has already passed.

Two. Forgiving contains an element of magic. It can't be controlled, but, under certain conditions, it will appear. And when it appears, we feel it in our body. Something that is almost a "thing" leaves the body. The muscular tension that we have habitually lived with eases. We're less vulnerable to infections and serious illness. The immune system improves. The face relaxes. Food tastes better. Depression diminishes. We feel lighter, physically lighter. There's also a change in our emotions. Anger changes to sorrow or regret. Rage diminishes. We become more available to other people, and more available to ourselves. Yet we think about ourselves less.

Forgiving isn't rational

When someone has harmed us — has hurt us, offended us, wounded us, abused us, there's no reason why we should let those offenses go. There's also no reason we should hope that the other person would. There's no rational reason that we should have any compassion for that person. Because forgiving isn't rational, there's no easy way to put forgiveness into practice. It's an act that says: "I will go on loving the life in you, or the divine in you, or the soul in you, even when I totally abhor what was done."

Here, we can begin to see that forgiveness is a spiritual act, and something even more. It's so very, very difficult because it requires a movement in consciousness, a vertical movement into a new level of consciousness. It often takes so long for forgiving to occur because it involves an initiation into a higher consciousness. Forgiveness, thus, isn't a one-time, one-moment act. It's a spiritual path.

Forgiving is not condoning

One. Forgiving is very disturbing. There's not a speck of sentimentality to it. Forgiving in no way justifies the actions that wound us. We don't have to seek out those who harmed us to let them know of our forgiveness.

Two. We don't forgive out of weakness. Also, we're not saying that what was done no longer matters. There's no need to deny, minimize, or make excuses for what was done. In fact, I may see the harm even more vividly and have stronger feelings about it.

Three. The intention to forgive sets two things in motion: An understanding that I can learn from my suffering and, secondly, that persons who inflict harm are no less and no more deserving of love than I am. For the rational mind, these two things don't make sense. However, much evidence that the person who has committed harm may not be able to feel love, or to feel at all.

Here, though, is where we have to take particular care in our experiential description of forgiveness. Because those who do serious harm often don't feel love and don't feel at all, there's a strong tendency to excuse their actions by suggesting that they acted out of pathology, a psychological illness. This tactic would be a mistake.

The "incubation period" of forgiveness

The first attempt at forgiveness often seems far beyond us. We know we need to be able to forget about the matter to some degree, albeit not completely. Certainly, it needs to cease to occupy our thoughts ceaselessly. We also have to be able to refrain from actively wishing the other person harm. And we have to be able to feel we can be patient with ourselves.

Thus, waiting is crucial in forgiveness. Events have to "settle" so that we can return to them in new ways.

Allowing events to settle also means that they can move from our head to our heart. This is extremely important because the heart is the point from which forgiveness emerges. However, it's not just a feeling; it's a spiritual act that epitomizes the healing power of love. It can no longer function as a judgment concerning who was right or wrong. False forgiveness doesn't bring healing; in fact, it adds to the original injury by intensifying the negative bond we have with the person who harmed us.

Responsibility and the forgiveness process

One. The process of forgiveness gains momentum when a new understanding of responsibility arises. We can't be forgiving as long as we only see the failings and faults of others. We have to first acknowledge who we are. This is an initiation process.

Two. At this juncture, we can lose our way. Specifically, we can understand that those who have harmed us: lack empathy; lack an inner sense of security; probably were brought up without love or understanding; and were themselves harmed by violence, hatred, and fear. Thus, it may seem that the person isn't to blame for the harm they did.

This kind thinking is prevalent in our current — highly superficial — culture.

Three. The psychological understanding outlined above doesn't encompass an accurate understanding of the nature of choice. There are innumerable moments in our life when we realize that we're choosing between treating someone with care or harming him or her. When we choose to harm, we also harm ourselves.

And, unless some kind of conscious work goes on to undo this effect — which is a "dulling" or a "numbing" — it will make us less conscious of our actions. When this happens, is such a person psychologically ill and not responsible?

Regardless of how we were treated in our upbringing, whether our parents were loving or not, the conscious choices we make in each moment remain a crucial factor. People who do harm can't be excused for their actions by saying: it was their shadow side; they're stuck at a schizoid level; they're unintegrated; they're sociopathic; they were harmed by their parents and are passing their pathology on. It *is* highly likely, though, that people who harm others are unconscious of what they're doing. The sadistic side of a person is satisfied only what it can see what it does and witnesses the effect. This side of us can be felt and even seen as if alongside our more 'normal' way of being.

Four. When we condone what someone has done because of a superficial psychological culture, then we're colluding with perpetrators of harm! We play into the notion that their behavior was inevitable, stemming from a history that can't be changed. But, this superficial psychologizing misses the fact that, unless one is genuinely psychotic or psychopathic, one *does* witness what one does and sees its effects. We remain responsible for our actions.

Five. We need a new framework for speaking about why people

harm others. In previous times, the framework was sin. We can't re-introduce that framework without a complete re-visioning of sin because the arbiters of what counts as sin — the clergy — have used this category for their own purposes. Organized religion has used the notion of sin to commit its own sins without shame.

Six. Regardless of psychological ramifications, harming others carries within it a moral aspect. It's an act of individual spirit-against-spirit. It's shocking to recognize that we can use the most salient aspect of our being against another.

That's the primary harm done when we injure others. It's not the physical hurt, the embarrassment, not even the abuse per se, without accountability.

It's that we use our spirit to commit harm to another. If harm didn't have this quality, then it would simply be a matter of psychological imbalance. It's not. Thus, in a new, spiritual psychology, it's important to understand how acts of harm towards others can truly be healed. And there are only two ways: Forgiveness and acknowledgment by the wrongdoer, followed by remorse, reparation, and petitions for forgiveness. It must be emphasized strongly, however, that for healing to occur, only the first — that is forgiveness — is needed. Also, we badly need a new, spiritual psychology of remorse, reparation, petition, and atonement. For example, remorse can be healthy, but it's often unhealthy because it brings guilt and shame rather than an awareness of the person who was harmed. In short, it gets "stuck" at the level of oneself.

What forgiveness does

One. A description of the experience: "It was an absolute release. It was forgiveness. I experienced it like a liquid feeling that embalmed me, like grace pouring over me. You can't make that happen. I felt like I was being anointed.

I'm able to see that I learned a lot, and I felt a real advancement of my soul — and I thought that if I die tomorrow, this has been resolved."

Two. The opposite of forgiveness is self-destructiveness. This person expresses the following: "For me, being in a state of unforgiveness was very self-destructive. It made me want to destroy my own life. It was a crisis that threw me headlong into despair and I was in that space for five or six years. I couldn't go on like that. In that time, I got diabetes. I'd given up hope.

Or: "I've become sharper than I was. I can be very analytical, almost harsh. I'm no longer idealizing, nor am I projecting pain outwards and blaming. On a daily basis, if something irritates me, I'm not forgiving. Having experienced forgiveness doesn't mean I have ceased to be judgmental!" Forgiveness concerns ongoing qualities of soul, not a singular act.

Three. Forgiveness brings us into Life and we realize that we don't come into the world entitled to anything. At the very heart of forgiveness is an inability to forgive Life itself for not giving us what we think. Whatever we receive beyond the content of living itself is the sense of Life, the great container of the contents of life, the luxurious presence of the gifts of the spiritual world, which are always present and seldom felt or perceived. We give up the fantasy that we can have the world be as we would like it. We find the means within ourselves to make up for what is lacking through contemplative presence rather than blaming others.

When we're not forgiving Life for not giving us what we want, we open up emptiness, deprivation, and depression.

Four. The growth movement concept --- which involves making life as you want it through the power of affirmations, visualizations, or expecting mysterious changes — is very egocentric.

Giving up is not surrendering

One. The art of forgiving is giving up our fantasies of what life is supposed to be without surrendering ourselves to whatever comes to us. How to do this? What is the practice:

Withdraw your attention from the person who has hurt you and return it to yourself and whoever else is in your care;
Take your attention from the past and bring it into the present
         moment.
Give up the illusion that your suffering will ultimatelyaffect the person who has harmed you and teach any meaningful lesson to that person. Abandon that person to his/her fate and abandon the desire to change that fate.

Two. Giving up is sometimes a forgetting. And, for many, this forgetting has to precede forgiveness. In this context, forgetting doesn't mean pretending nothing happened. It means living without those events being perpetually in your mind. This forgetting process prepares the ground for giving up fantasies of what life is supposed to be. This forgetting also means we can wake up and not be immediately troubled by what has happened to us. Sometimes, this will only occur for an hour or a week; being relatively secure that painful memories won't intrude; being able to go to sleep. This kind of forgetting allows a psychological "scab" to form over an open emotional wound. This is healthy! It's healthy because it restores our senses, which have been enormously disturbed after harm is inflicted. It allows the return of our capacity to give attention to the world. The 'scab' gradually dissolves.

The core of forgiveness

Forgiveness doesn't involve condoning, trivializing, minimizing, ignoring, or pretending to forget what has happened. It also doesn't withdraw blame. It *does*, however, make it clearer that we can't absent ourselves from the events that happened. Anger isn't necessarily abandoned, but vengeance is. We often talk about forgiveness in such a way that it sounds like we're giving something away when we forgive or that we accept something when someone forgives us.

Forgiveness doesn't take anything away. Instead, it restores us to our spirit!

When our spirit is again with us, we realize something about the one who has perpetrated harm: *We are one and the same*. This sameness is sameness in spirit only. We're both embodied spirit-beings. You are the same in your unchanging spirit as I. As spirit-beings, we both share: fears of suffering loss, the need for respect, the yearning for acceptance and love. Also, paradoxically, our connections with others are closer when they remain less personal. I am in my unchanging spirit.

As long as my connection with one who has harmed me is personal -- if, for instance, I think I'm supposed to love this person because he or she is a parent, a lover, a wife, husband, friend, or employer who has harmed me, then I am bound to that person. And, as long as I can't relinquish all of the anger, rage, and memories, then I remain in a negative bond with this person. Similarly, if I wholly forget what has occurred, it will come out in a bodily way, as a symptom.

Ultimately, forgiveness is the extraordinary capacity to be close to one who has harmed us — and its transformative loveliness emerges as closeness, even oneness, of spirit.

Acknowledgments

I am grateful to Ann-Marie Fryer Wiboltt for transcribing this monograph from working notes.

Printed in Great Britain
by Amazon